Contagious Joy

Brian Richardson

ISBN: 978-1-914173-03-5

www.lifepublications.org.uk

Acknowledgements

With grateful thanks to
Christopher and Christine Harnetty
for all their friendship, help and support.

Dedication

To Lois, Mark, Paul, Sara, Anna
and
my seven grandchildren
who bring me great joy.

Contents

You love Him passionately although you do not see Him, but through believing in Him you are saturated with an ecstatic joy, indescribably sublime and immersed in glory. For you are reaping the harvest of your faith – the full salvation promised you – your souls' victory.

1 Peter 1:8-9

There is no virtue in the Christian life which is not made radiant with joy; there is no circumstance and no occasion which is not illuminated with joy. A joyless life is not a Christian life, for joy is one constant recipe for Christian living.

William Barclay

Introduction

He has made me glad and no one can make me sad.
He makes me shout and no one can make me doubt.
He it is that makes me dance and leap and there is no
one that can keep down my feet.

Billy Bray

Such a deep-seated joy, unspeakable and full of
glory, is an emotion we cannot produce. It comes to
us from God for *the fruit of the Spirit is...joy.*
Galatians 5:22

Herbert Lockyer

I have no intention of being a misery in my old age, (although I am sorely tempted at times). It is amazing when your body starts to wear out how many things you can find to moan and complain about. One of the reasons I am writing this book is the hope that by the time I come to writing the last page, I will know something of the amazing joy of the Lord myself.

My greatest hope is that precious brothers and sisters who read this book will be inspired to enter into this *"joy unspeakable and full of glory"* and gain a revelation that we Christians should be the happiest people on the face of this planet. We who follow the King should be the envy of the world because we have such an inward joy that makes us shout, dance and sing. We who own allegiance to *The Lord of the Dance* must be instruments in His hand to bring some joy into this miserable old world.

Looking through the hundreds of Christian books in my library, I do not have one that focuses on joy, not even a chapter! (Maybe it's my bad choice.) When I commenced this book, I knew that joy was a theme that runs right through the Scriptures, but as I have begun to write I have received an increasing revelation of how much exuberant joy is to be found in Him.

People's names in the Bible always have some significance, and it is interesting to see that one of the tribes of Israel is called 'Asher', which means 'happy'. Surely our journey in Christ should be a pathway of bliss.

If, as CS Lewis says, "Joy is the serious business of heaven," we need to make a serious study as to how this fruit of the Spirit will manifest itself. It is not my intention in this book to suggest, "Do these six things and the joy of the Lord will be yours!" Joy is always a by-product and must never be your focus in life.

When I was a lad at Grammar School in Leyton back in the early 1950s, I belonged to the Science Club, mainly because they arranged all kinds of interesting outings. I shall never forget our visit to a local Gas Works, it was in the days before North Sea gas, so it was a works that produced Town Gas made from coal. What has remained in my memory from that visit all those years ago, is all the wonderful by-products that were obtained by extracting gas from coal. From those by-products came such finished items as nylon stockings, Aspirin, plus many others. The main purpose of that Gas Works was to produce gas, but there were so many by-products. Our main purpose in life is, "To know Him and enjoy Him forever", and one of the incredible by-products of enjoying our relationship with Him is, "The joy of the Lord".

As Alexander MacLaren said,

> "To pursue joy is to lose it. The only way to get it is to follow steadily the path of duty, without thinking of joy, and then, like sheep, it comes most surely

> unsought, and we 'being in the way', the angel of God, bright-haired joy, is sure to meet us."

Joy is part of the nine-fold fruit of the Spirit, and a tree does not struggle and strive to produce fruit, it simply and quietly bares fruit, and as we abide in the vine so shall we. The book of Romans expresses the thought that joy is a major part of the Kingdom of God (where Jesus rules).

> *For the Kingdom of God is not eating and drinking, but righteousness and peace and **joy** in the Holy Spirit. Romans 14:17*

I am fully aware that there is incredible sorrow, pain and suffering in this world, and I am in no way denying the reality of sorrow, there is so much in this present world to be sorrowful about. But Paul writes,

> *As sorrowful, **yet always rejoicing**.*
>
> *2 Corinthians 6:10.*

It is possible for both emotions to live together. I try to elaborate further on this verse in my book *Your Kingdom Come*. I am in no way trying to deny that sorrow is part of life, but that for the Lord's own, joy should be the dominant note. Making Jesus Lord of your life does not mean we join the "misery brigade".

When pollster George Barna asked the question in a national survey in the USA, "If you could ask God one question, what would you ask Him?" The greatest response was, "Why is there pain and suffering in this world?" So many great books have been written giving us some insight and understanding on this subject of pain and suffering, but there seems to be few books on joy, hence, here we go!

Brian

If you have no joy, there's a leak in your Christianity somewhere.

Billy Sunday

1

The Joy of the Lord

God has poured out the oil of bliss on you more than any of your friends.

Hebrews 1:9 tPt

The Oxford dictionary definition of the word "joy" is, "a vivid emotion of pleasure". Our God is a God of great emotion and one of those emotions is "joy". The Creator has made us in His image so that we too can have this same ability to experience this "vivid emotion of pleasure".

In 2019, 26% of the adult population attended a music festival somewhere in the UK. (50% of that number would have been under twenty years of age.) Many felt that, to them, it was a greater priority to go to a music festival than going on holiday. Certainly they would not spend all that time and money (£2.6 billion) if they did not find some joy in going to those concerts; although, observing some on their return home, having slept less than four hours a night and consumed copious amounts of alcohol, they do not seem to be that chirpy! Some of the attendees needing a "sickie" from work or college to recover!

God has obviously given mankind this wonderful ability to enjoy life, yet *"The joy of the Lord"* is something far deeper than the passing joy of a music festival. It is more than the joy of getting together with a few pals and having a good laugh.

I love a good laugh as much as any man or woman, and I know God has a very acute sense of humour (not that I always understand His jokes), but the Holy Trinity's joy is a much deeper thing than mere laughter. As the Roman philosopher Seneca said at the time of Christ, "True joy is a serene and sober motion; they are miserably out that take laughing for rejoicing: the seat of it is within, and there is no cheerfulness like the resolutions of a brave mind, that has fortune under its feet."

The rivers of God's joy run still and very deep indeed.

> Joy is distinctly a Christian word and a Christian thing. It is the reverse of happiness. Happiness is the result of what happens of an agreeable sort. Joy has its springs deep down inside. And that spring never runs dry, no matter what happens. Only Jesus gives that joy. He had joy, singing its music within, even under the shadow of the cross.
>
> SD Gordon

As we read John's Gospel, Jesus is about to go to the cross and make the ultimate sacrifice for our sakes, the shadow of Gethsemane lay before Him, the tsunami waves of God's judgement for humanity's sins and rebellion are about to crash down over Him, and so He gathers His disciples together for a last meal together.

He has so much to say to them before He leaves them, and then, in the midst of it all, He adds,

> *These things I have spoken to you, that **my joy** may remain in you, and that **your joy** might be full.*
>
> *John 15:11*

Later, He adds,

> *Ask and you will receive, that **your joy** may be full.*
>
> *John 16:24*

And then again,

> *These things I speak...that they may have **My joy** fulfilled in themselves.*
>
> *John 17:13*

The Lord's joy must be something other than mere human joy, for after His cruel death, it was written of the mourners that they ate their meals *"with gladness of heart praising God"*. Later, when they were in more difficult circumstances, they spent their time singing, whether facing death in the Colosseum in Rome or in prison. Paul and Silas sang all night in the darkness of their prison cell, with their backs bleeding and torn, because Christ's joy was theirs. His promise was fulfilled in them.

This joy was not to be had one moment and then lost when crushing tragedy came. If so, it would have made tragedy more powerful than joy. Jesus came to give us victory over hell itself. When Jesus took the horror of the cross and made it a victory, He provided the same victory over our problems, no matter how great or ominous.

I remember one very dark season in my life when I was assailed by so many problems, with family, finance, church and relationships. I felt incredibly low and worthless. I jumped in my car and drove some twenty-five miles to some parkland in Essex just to escape the bleak situation, which was oppressing me. As I climbed out of the car, it was as though I had stepped into heaven, such joy overcame me that I leapt and danced and shouted for the sheer joy of being alive. God in His great mercy visited me with His joy, and I went home a changed man.

The joy of the Lord is not extracted from surrounding circumstances.

For many their joy is distilled from their circumstances, and therefore, if those circumstances be adverse, they are destitute of happiness. Joy can be like honey gathered from every opened flower and we flit like bees from one to another finding more in some than others. But what were Christ's surroundings when He spoke about His joy? Poverty – reproach – betrayal – anticipated agony and death. His joy came from somewhere else other than His circumstances. The source of His joy was deep within His soul. *The joys of this world flow into us via our five senses, but the joy of the Lord is something that flows out of the soul.*

Here lies the difference between the child of God and the child of this world. Yes, like the world, we can enjoy the beauty of a flower, a country scene, an amazing sunset, or a child's smiling face; we can be enthralled by the sound of music. We drink in the scent of a rose, enjoy a lovely meal, delight in the company of friends, all these things Jesus and His followers enjoyed too, but the joy of the heart is independent of all these, it comes from within and we can carry it with us whatever the outward circumstances.

The joy of the Lord is the joy of communion with the Father.

Jesus ever had an abiding sense of His Father's nearness, and deep beyond all description must have been the fellowship between them. In John 16:32 Jesus is speaking of His betrayal in the immediate future,

> *Indeed the hour is coming, yes has now come, that you will be scattered, each to his own, and will leave me alone. And yet I am not alone, because the Father is with me.*

Here is one of His fountains of joy. Who could ever give words to express what joy the Father, the Holy Spirit and the Son shared together?

Nevertheless, the Father of the Lord Jesus Christ is our Father too! He who communed with our Elder Brother will commune with the younger brother too!

How many of us ancients who were around in the 1950s loved to hear George Beverley Shea sing in the Billy Graham Crusades and especially when he sang the ballad, *I Walked In The Garden Alone*, the chorus goes,

He walks with me and He talks with me
And tells me I am His own,
And the joy we share as we tarry there
None other has ever known.

The joy of communion with the Father.

It is strange how different songs move different people. There is one hymn that I have rarely sung that has not brought a lump into my throat and tears in my eyes. It was written about 150 years ago in India by Ellen Lakshmi Goreh.

In The Secret of His Presence

In the secret of His presence
How my soul delights to hide!
Oh, how precious are the lessons
Which I learn at Jesus' side!
Earthly cares can never vex me,
Neither trials lay me low;
For when Satan comes to tempt me,
To the secret place I go.

Contagious Joy

When my soul is faint and thirsty,
'Neath the shadow of His wing
There is cool and pleasant shelter
And a fresh and crystal spring;
And my Saviour rests beside me
As we hold communion sweet;
If I tried I could not utter
What He says when thus we meet.

Only this I know: I tell Him
All my doubts and griefs and fears;
Oh, how patiently He listens!
And my drooping soul He cheers:
Do you think He ne'er reproves me?
What a false friend He would be,
If He never, never told me
Of the sins which He must see!

Would you like to know the sweetness
Of the secret of the Lord?
Go and hide beneath His shadow;
This shall then be your reward;
And when'er you leave the silence
Of that happy meeting place,
You will bear the shining image
Of the Master on your face.

The joy of communion! To know every day, in all circumstances 24/7 that He is there in the good, bad and indifferent times, is so amazing. At the bedside of the parent who has just passed away; at the moment when your wife is just to give birth and the lives of mother and baby hang in the balance; when you are about to submit yourself to the surgeon's knife, and have to sign a form first that says, you are ready for the risk that he might mess it up this time as he did yesterday!

Have you ever had a "dark night of the soul"? I certainly have, where I have even contemplated stopping the world and getting off, because of the misunderstanding, wrong judgement and rejection of others. And yet God has been there!

Vanessa and I, in pursuing our ministry, drive at least 30,000 miles per year. One year I drove over 50,000 miles. Over the sixty years of driving in UK, Europe and the Americas, I have experienced three near fatal accidents, twice on the motorway, twice the car was "a write-off" and each time I came out of those crashes without a scratch. God was there!

It is said the three greatest traumas in our life in the Western world are losing your spouse, changing your job, and buying and selling a house. At one period of my life I had to face all three at the same time. How wonderful to know the Father is there with you through it all.

The joy of realised and returned love

Jesus felt the love of the Father, He declares, *The Father loves the Son.* And He loved the Father, He said, *I love the Father.*

There is a beautiful spot on North Devon called Watersmeet. It is where the East Lyn River and the Hoar Oak Water meet. They both come leaping and roaring along channels filled with boulders and rocks, and each is as beautiful as the other, you can look at either with equal delight. Both are born from the clouds, both bright and sparkling, yet they both come from different parts of Exmoor. For many miles they run their different merry course until they flow into one another, and great is the water's music as they meet and dance together and go on their joyful way together.

And so we have two streams; one is called the **"Father loves me"** and the other is called **"I love the Father"**, both are born from above, one from the high mountain of the Father's

House and the other from the Rock of Ages. And the music of the meeting is sheer joy! Reader, why don't you pause right now and enjoy the Father's love?

My wife, Vanessa, and I not only celebrate our wedding anniversary, but also the day when we had our first kiss after I had asked her if she would go out with me and she said, "Yes". That day and in the days that followed, I was the happiest man on the planet. The joy of realised and returned love! To me there is no greater success in life than to know that you know that you know, you are loved by the Father.

So dear, so very dear to God,
More dear I cannot be.
The love wherewith He loves the Son,
Such is His love for me.

This is the great joy of being a Christian, to be in a relationship with the greatest lover in the universe. It makes your heart sing.

The joy of complete surrender

Jesus and His disciples arrive at Jacob's Well in the town of Samaria; they are all tired and hungry, especially Jesus. The disciples say to their Rabbi, "Wait here, we will go and buy a 'take away'". Samaria was not a safe place for Jews, so they all went together, leaving Jesus by the well. (I guess they thought that there might be some safety in numbers.)

We all know the ensuing story of Jesus' encounter with the woman from Samaria and her response to Him. When the disciples return, they look at Jesus, and, to their amazement, it looked as if He had been eating while they were away, He looked so revived and refreshed; so they asked one another the question, "Has someone fed Him whilst we've been gone?" to which Jesus replied,

The Joy of the Lord

I have food to eat of which you do not know. My food is to do the will of Him who sent me, and to finish the work.

John 4:34

Doing the Father's will was His meat and drink; it was His luxury, His great joy.

I remember a senior Pastor sighing to me one day, referring to many of the visiting speakers who had spoken at the church, "Everyone seems to have their own agenda." Even the greatest amongst us at times can have mixed motivations for the things we do. Oh! To be fully surrendered to the Father's will, finding our greatest delight in doing His will.

The reason for so many miseries in church life is because they are resisting His will. It is the clashing with the Father's will that is the cause of so much disquiet and frustration in the body of Christ.

Submitting to the Father's will is what we were made for in the first place, and when we do otherwise, we only do damage. It is like using a chisel to knock in a nail, or a hammer to cut a hole in a piece of wood, you might just about succeed, but what damage would be done to the chisel, nail and the surrounding woodwork!

Madame Marie Guyon, the Christian mystic of the seventeenth century, who spent eight years in prison for her beliefs wrote,

"While place we seek or place we shun,
The soul finds happiness in none;
But with a God to guide our way,
Tis equal joy to go or stay."

The joy of complete surrender!

The joy of looking back on a life's work finished

Jesus said,

> *"I have finished the work you gave me to do."*
> *John 17:4*

There is such a great joy and satisfaction in a job well done. Every time I look out of our living room sliding doors into our back garden, I see a patio that I laid a couple of years ago and think to myself, "That looks so good. That was such a splendid addition to the aspect of the garden." I then lift my eyes and look at the rockery with its little stream and rock pools that I created last year and think, "That is such a beautiful improvement to that corner of the garden." A job well done! I trust there will come a day when I hold this book in my hands as a published item and feel it was worth all those hours in front of the computer.

Paul says,

> *"I have fought the good fight, I have finished the race, I have kept the faith."*
> *2 Timothy 4:7*

None of us can feel fully satisfied with our lives; we know we could have served the Lord so much better, more often, more consistently, more wholeheartedly, that we must have missed the mark so often. Yet, there is joy in serving Jesus, a great joy in doing what you know He wants you to do; such a joy of being where God wants you to be. For over 15 years I ministered in Barking, East London, and I often used to say to my congregation, "Why be in Bermuda if God wants you in Barking?" I love the words of Solomon,

> *"The end of the thing is better than its beginning."*
> *Ecclesiastes 7:8*

We may not have started very well, but by His grace we can all finish well.

Perhaps Jack W Hayford puts it much better in his book *Building The Real You*,

> Joy is the discovery that everything you dreamed true fulfilment would be has already been planned for you by God Himself, and that He is ready to bring it about – for you and in you.

The joy of approaching glory

And now I come to you *– John 17:13*

In a few hours, the Sun of righteousness would set in blood and then would rise to set no more.

The joy that had been set before Him for years, that had nerved Him to endure the cross and despise the shame was now at hand. **"I to you".**

Our loving Lord, ever mindful of His disciples, prays that they may have the same joyful anticipation of nearing glory.

> *Joy inexpressible and full of glory.*
>
> *1 Peter 1:8*

The writer to the Hebrews pens,

> *Knowing in yourselves that you have in heaven a better and enduring substance.*
>
> *Hebrews 10:14*

Our substance here is very unsubstantial; there is no substance to it! But God has given us a promise of real estate in Glory. **We know in ourselves** that we have an enduring substance in heaven. Heaven, even now, is ours, we have the title deeds, we have the earnest of it, we have the fruits of it. We have heaven in price, in principle and in promise. This we know not just because we read it in the Bible or heard it from the pulpit, but **"in ourselves."**

Thank God we may have, and do have, the joy of an inheritance in heaven! Christ's joy is our joy, His heaven our heaven, His home our home.

My joy fulfilled in themselves.
John 17:13

2

The Joy of Creation

A joyous God fills the universe. Joy is the ultimate word describing God and His world. Creation was an act of joy, of delight in the goodness of what was done.

Dallas Willard

Vanessa and I have the great privilege and joy of living just off the Chiltern Hills, officially designated as an 'Area of Natural Outstanding Beauty'. We moved seventeen years ago to the area, because of our love of walking in this breath-taking countryside. One day, after a hectic and pressurised two weeks, we took a day off and walked through 'The Golden Valley' in Ashridge Forest. As we stopped for a picnic lunch, we just drunk in the stunning beauty of the scene, no noise of traffic, no sign of human activity, we were made whole as we listened to the birds singing and the call of the pheasant in the distance. Earlier on in our walk we saw so many grazing fallow deer that we lost count; it was all quite inebriating.

I thought, if we can so delight and joy in His creation, how much more must the great Creator who expresses His thoughts by making flowers?

Dr Brian Simmonds, in his Passion translation of the Bible, tells us that the Hebrew word that is usually translated for us in our Bibles as "born" (or brought forth) means "to kick and twirl" or "to dance." Dr Simmonds then explains that the word "rejoicing" in Proverbs 8:30 can also be translated as "joyfully playing" or "laughing". Dr Simmonds goes on to say,

> Christ's part in creation filled out in Proverbs 8: *"I was there dancing"*, He cries (v24). Have you ever thought of the Trinity "dancing together" as they brought all things into existence? What a picture! Before everything was made – from ocean depths to the sculpted mountains – Christ performed the role of Master Artist, playfully fashioning the earth and the heavens with laughter and joy, finding his delight in the children of men (our first parents, Adam and Eve).

The Trinity dancing together

We all have problems trying to comprehend the Trinity, but then a God who our tiny minds could comprehend would be a tiny God indeed! As Timothy Keller says, "The doctrine of the Trinity overloads our mental circuits." Of all the world faiths, Christianity is the only one that teaches that God is a Trinity; one God who exists eternally in three persons Father, Son and Holy Spirit.

If God were just one being in eternity, before creation, all he could do would be to focus on Himself. Of necessity He would be self-centred. He therefore could be all powerful, but He could not be all loving, for love is self-giving and He would have none to whom He could give Himself. As Timothy Keller points out, the life of the…

> Trinity is characterised not by self-centredness, but by mutually self-giving love. When we delight and serve someone else, we enter into a dynamic orbit around him or her, we centre on the interests and desires of the other. That creates a dance, particularly if there are three persons, each of whom moves around the other two. So it is, the Bible tells us. Each of the divine persons centres upon the others. None demands the others revolve around him. Each voluntarily circles the other two, pouring love, delight and adoration into them. Each person of the Trinity loves, defers to, and rejoices in the others. That creates a dynamic, pulsating dance of joy and love.

Such was their joy and delight in the dance that they wanted to share this joy, so they created the heavenly host with angel and archangel to join in with them in the dance and so they all gave themselves to one another with exuberant joy. Then as mentioned above they created the universe to enlarge the dance and the delight for one another and create a kind of explosion of glory. We read in Job 38:7 that at creation,

> *The morning stars sang together, and all the sons of God shouted for joy.*

It all became one great dance of joy.

I love gardening; it has been a hobby of mine since I was a teenager. By late May early June, the garden is at its peak with a profusion of bloom which delights my heart, but my joy is doubled when my wife enjoys it with me. But my supreme enjoyment is, when friends come to visit, and they go into the garden and soak up the beauty. It must be something like that for the Trinity as they gaze upon their creation, a joy shared.

Contagious Joy

God has made us in His own image, so that as creators who enjoy creating, we can share and expand that joy as we share the fruits of our toil with others.

Love's heart is to share and so the Trinity crowned creation by making man to join the dance. But, the great and terrible fall of man which caused man to centre life around himself instead of God and others, created the opportunity for the Trinity to make the greatest love-sacrifice, self-giving act of all at Calvary, so that we can once again join the dance. In fact,

> *The earnest expectation of the creation eagerly waits for the revealing of the sons of God.*
>
> *Romans 8:12*

> Behind the universe and the human race lies the astonishing philanthropy of the Triune God. In sheer grace the Father, Son and Spirit have chosen not to live out their great 'dance of life' without us. They have chosen not to hoard their glory, but to share it, to share their fellowship and camaraderie, their love and laughter, their creativity and dignity and excellence with us, to live it all out in union with the human race.

C. Baxter Kruger

Holy Spirit, in Your amazing grace, teach us how to respond to the invitation and take Your hand and join the dance with a joy unspeakable and full of glory!

3

The Joy of His Presence

In Your presence there is fullness of joy; at Your right hand are pleasures for evermore.

Psalm 16:11

The Holy Spirit turns to joy whatever He touches.

St Seraphim of Sarov 1754-1833

One of the greatest, most positive experiences in this world is the overwhelming joy in something or a person. It is said that for God to create the heart of a mother's love for her children, He must have such a passion in His own heart. It follows therefore, for exuberant overwhelming joy to exist in this universe, it must first have already been in the heart of God in the first place. The Trinity must be the happiest persons in the universe, and for many of us the most ecstatic experiences we ever enjoy are found in His presence. That is why the psalmist sings,

> *In His presence there is fullness of joy; at Your right hand pleasures for evermore.*
>
> *Psalm 16:11*

The psalms ring with the sound of joyous praise from beginning to end.

Contagious Joy

In His presence there is no place for negativity or evil, no place for fear or doubt, only joyous freedom.

Most Christians with any depth of relationship with the Saviour, will confess that when they have considered some of their greatest experiences of God's presence that they have ever had, will remember besides the awe and great ecstasy, an overwhelming joy of the moment. That is why when God turns up and manifests His presence in some gatherings of believers, nobody wants to go home. Many of us will have read stories of great revivals in history of how, when God's presence was manifest, the meetings often went on through the night, nobody wanted to go home, although they had to go to work next morning.

> A genuine revival without joy in the Lord is as impossible as spring without flowers, or day-dawn without light.
>
> Charles H Spurgeon

Dr Michael Brown, who has studied and immersed himself in revival, said, "Why is there water in the ocean? Revival without joy would be unthinkable."

Grawys Jones, a Pastor in the Welsh Revival of 1904/5 wrote,

> Out on the roads I could hear companies of people going down to Aberdare and singing. Companies going to the east and to the north and to Cwmdare. About 4 o'clock I went home and I could hear companies in the early morning singing with all their might. I went to bed, but could hardly sleep, and when I did, I was laughing for joy in my sleep and I got up in the morning full of joy.
>
> *Carriers of the Fire* by Karen Lowe

We were very blessed to be involved with what became known affectionately as the "Toronto Outpouring" in 1994. We had the privilege to travel to Toronto to some of those early meetings and later to see the same kind of outpouring in London. The Presence of God was so real that people danced and jumped for joy, many overcome with laughter did not know how to contain themselves as the joy of the Lord overcame them. We witnessed at that time so many transformed lives as the joy of the Lord set them free from physical and psychological sicknesses; we saw families reconciled, lapsed Christians restored. I always remember one older lady that attended the church who always came through the door with such a miserable look on her face, but one day the joy of the Lord hit her and ever after she came to church with a great big beam of joy on her face, completely transformed.

Psalm 16:11 was worked out in front of our eyes. Many miraculous healings, even dead brain cells resurrected in His joyous presence. People carried the joy out on to the street, to the local bus stops and restaurants and as a result folks came into the church building to find out what was making people so deliriously happy. They soon found themselves caught up by the mighty presence of God and they too became drunk with the "new wine".

AW Tozer wrote,

> When we give the Holy Spirit His place, there will be joy that doesn't have to be worked up. It will be a joy that springs like a fountain, an artesian well that springs from within. That's one characteristic of a Spirit-filled congregation. They will be a joyful people, and it will be easy to distinguish them from the children of the world.

In Acts 8, Philip hits Samaria and a revival breaks out and we read,

> *So there was great joy in the city.*
>
> *Acts 8:8*

As William Vander Hoven said, "Joy is not the absence of trouble, but the presence of Christ."

And the Apostle Paul says,

> *The Kingdom of God is not eating and drinking, but righteousness and peace and* ***joy in the Holy Spirit****.*
>
> *Romans 14:17*

When Jesus walked this earth, He was continually thronged by people. I believe it was more than His teaching, more than the miracles, more than the aura of His dynamic presence; they found a joyous freedom in His presence that they could never find anywhere else in this world. There are many people in this world who are no fun to be with, so we tend to avoid their company if we can. Not so Jesus, He was a coveted guest at weddings, children sought His company; the crowds continually surrounded Him. Some picture Jesus like Mr Spock from Star Trek, completely devoid of emotions especially laughter,

> *But God anointed Him with the oil of gladness more than your companions.*
>
> *Hebrews 1:8*

What was it that caused King David to dance for joy as he brought the Ark of the Covenant back to Jerusalem? Surely it was more than an accomplishment of a dream, more than the successful transit of this precious piece of furniture to his capital city? I like to think it was the Presence in the Ark that caused his feet to dance? Like Billy Bray, it was the "Presence" that made him dance and leap, and there was no one, including David's wife Michal, that could keep down his feet.

It's a wonderful thing when the joy reaches the feet, Merlin Carothers in his well-known book *Praise Works*, tells how one day as he stood on the beach communing with God, suddenly, he was so filled with the joy of the Lord that he said, "My feet have got the message", and started to dance.

> ***Joy is more divine than sorrow, for joy is bread and sorrow is medicine.***
>
> ***H W Beecher***

Every virtue divorced from thankfulness is maimed and limps along the spiritual road.
John Henry Jowett

4

The Joy of Thankfulness

In everything give thanks; for this is the will of God in Christ Jesus for you.
1 Thessalonians 5:18

God's will, God's perfect plan is that we give thanks for everything, the good, the bad and the ugly, everything. Why? Because He commands us to be thankful, and He never asks us to do anything that He also does not give us the grace to do it.

He who calls you is faithful, who also will do it.
1 Thessalonians 5:24

As His children, He is at work in all our circumstances, He loves us, wants the very best for us and His thoughts are towards us all the time. He has our best interests at heart, so everything is working for our good somehow or other. I am not saying everything that comes our way is part of His plan, will and design, some things that happen are undoubtedly not His will, but **in it, through it, and beyond it He can work good.** He is our Fierce Protector and Pastor, so even when everything is seemingly against us and is going wrong, and it is very hard to see how any good can come out of a situation, He is still Lord over all. We discuss this aspect in greater depth in chapter 12, *The Joy of Tribulation.*

The Apostle Paul has an encounter with Jesus where the Lord downloads insight on the rite of communion,

> *For I received from the Lord...on the same night in which He was betrayed took bread;* ***and when He had given thanks****, He broke it and said, 'Take eat.'*
>
> 1 Corinthians 11:23,24

We need to see something amazing here, having touched on this passage already, the very night on which Jesus is betrayed, He gives thanks. In the midst of ultimate betrayal, He is thanking His Father in heaven. He doesn't tell us to just praise Him in hard times, He gives us the ultimate example to follow.

Beni Johnson writes in *The Power of Communion*,

> Thankfulness is one of the most vital attributes within reach of every person alive. If I could prayerfully lay hands on people and impart a thankful heart, without question, I would. And I would make that the single greatest focus of my life. An impartation of thankfulness would have the greatest impact on the hearts and minds of people. It would literally change the world as we know it.

Indeed, what a flood of joy would sweep the world.

One of the great keys to finding joy is in being thankful. Meet a thankful person, and you meet a happy person.

Songs so often have associations for us, sometimes of a set of circumstances, and other times, people. One such song to me is the old hymn *Count Your Blessings*. It was my mother-in-law's favourite and whenever it was sung, Mum, with her happy, placid nature came to mind. We always used to add a chorus at the end of the hymn...

Count your blessings, name them two by two.
Count your blessings, name them four by four.
Count your blessings, name them by the score.
And it will surprise you there are thousands more.

Over my sixty plus years of church experience, I have never heard a congregation sing that song without joy, and if we were to ask a person as they sang the words, "Did they feel any better for singing the hymn?" the answer would always have been in the affirmative.

Martin Luther, the great Protestant reformer, referring to the sin of worrying, says,

> I have one preacher that I love better than any other on earth; it is my little tame robin, who preaches to me daily. I put his crumbs upon my windowsill, especially at night. He hops on to the windowsill when he wants his supper and takes as much as he desires to satisfy his need. From thence he always hops to a little tree close by and lifts up his voice to God and sings his carols of praise and gratitude, tucks his little head under his wing and goes fast asleep, and leaves tomorrow to look after itself. He is the best preacher that I have on earth.

If you have nothing to be grateful for, make up your mind that there is something wrong with you and you need some serious counselling.

Shakespeare condemned unthankfulness, "Ingratitude, thou marble hearted fiend," from *King Lear*, and again in *As You Like It,*

Blow, blow, thou winter wind,
Thou art not so unkind
As man's ingratitude.

Contagious Joy

The Apostle Paul said that one evidence of godlessness, was being unthankful,

> *Neither were they thankful.*
> *Romans 1:21*

Those who belong to Lord can never give enough thanks. We are surrounded by His mercies – physical, material, temporal, spiritual. We can never thank Father, Son and Holy Spirit enough for the amazing gift of eternal life. It will take eternity to tell of our thanks!

One remembers when God miraculously delivered Israel from the Egyptians at the Red Sea, how they so rejoiced, sang and played their tambourines at their deliverance. Three days later they were moaning and complaining; it was their lack of thanksgiving and belief in the goodness of God that caused their downfall. I believe an evil spirit entered that nation at that moment, and for the next forty years they hardly ceased from their whining and complaining against God and Moses. They complained about the water, they complained about the food, they complained about the leadership. They were like the English, they could always find something to complain about. God said,

> *For forty years I was grieved with that generation. It is a people who go astray in their hearts, and they do not know my ways.*
> *Psalm 95:9-10*

At the time of writing this book, God taught me a salutary lesson about the importance of being thankful. After nearly twelve months without a proper break, we went away for five days on holiday, the weather was great and we richly enjoyed the wonderful Dorset countryside. On the way home, I started to complain that the holiday was all too short and that we needed another week to have a proper holiday, especially after all the confinement of the Corona Virus lockdown. I immediately became very depressed. I could not believe how low I felt. By my complaint I had given the devil a legal right to attack me and the next day I was so agitated that I felt I was on the edge of a mental breakdown. (Thankfully, I have never had such an experience, so I do not really know what it is like to be in such a dark place.)

Vanessa took me for a walk on a hill near our home and asked me a poignant question, "When did this darkness start?" Suddenly, I realised that God had given us a wonderful holiday break and blessed us in so many countless ways, and there I was, murmuring and complaining. I immediately asked for forgiveness and renounced my unbelief for doubting His great goodness. Like a flash my downcast spirit lifted, and I was my happy self again. A miracle of transformation in a matter of seconds! I trust that if I never forget that experience and learn to give thanks always in every situation, what a happy soul I will be.

I cannot end this chapter without quoting,

> *Enter into His gates with thanksgiving, and into His courts with praise. Be thankful to Him and bless His name.*
>
> *Psalm 100:4.*

The psalmist commences by exclaiming, ***Make a joyful shout to the Lord!*** And why? *We are His people the sheep of His pasture.* That is more than enough reason to shout His praise, and then the psalmist goes on to gives us even more cause to be thankful,

> *For the Lord is good; His mercy everlasting and His truth endures to all generations.*

The more we comprehend that the Lord is our Shepherd, the more joyful and thankful we will be. CH Spurgeon wrote,

> We have all things and abound; not because I have a good store in the bank, not because I have skill and wit with which to win my bread, but because the Lord is my shepherd.

Maybe if we all started our days declaring Psalm 100, we would all find ourselves and those around us in a happier frame of mind.

5

The Joy of Salvation

Oh, the joy of beholding the face of a reconciled God!

CH Spurgeon

Therefore with joy you will draw water from the wells of salvation.

Isaiah 12:3

Blessed are the people who know the joyful sound.

Psalm 89:15

We love the sound of music, the singing of the birds, children's laughter, but is there a sweeter sound to reach the inner ear of the soul than the voice of scripture saying to us, "Jesus saves!"? The joy of hearing how we can be emancipated from the guilt and power of sin and made new creatures in Christ is the greatest sound for a sinner on this earth to ever hear. Happy indeed, *are the people who hear the joyful sound.*

> The danger was never to exaggerate the gospel, but always to underestimate it. Something happened to mankind in Christ which is by far superior to what happened to mankind in Adam (Romans 5.18). And it happened without our permission!
>
> Francois du Toit

Contagious Joy

The Apostle Paul writes to the Romans, speaking of their hope in Christ,

> *What incredible joy bursts forth within us as we keep on celebrating our hope of experiencing God's glory!*
>
> *Romans 5:2 tPt,*

And then again,

> *And even more than that, we overflow with triumphant joy in our new relationship of living in harmony with God – all because of Jesus Christ!*
>
> *Romans 5:11 tPt*

Principal Rainy, of whom a child once remarked that she believed he went to heaven every night, because he was so happy every day, once used a fine metaphor about a Christian's joy. "Joy" he said, "is the flag which is flown from the castle of the heart when the King is in residence there."

So many of us experienced something of that joy when we first committed ourselves into the hands of Jesus and put our trust in His finished work on the cross.

Jesus, in His parable of the lost sheep says,

> *There will be more joy in heaven over one sinner who repents than over ninety nine just persons.*
>
> *Luke 15:7*

and again the parable of the lost coin,

> *There is joy in the presence of the angels of God over one sinner who repents.*
>
> *Luke 15:9*

If heaven rejoices, how much more should we rejoice? Jesus goes on to add, in the parable of the prodigal son, that when they began to be merry because his son who was lost was found, the Father says,

> *It was right that we should make merry and be glad.*
>
> *Luke 15:32*

"It was right!" and it is only right for us to be joyful in our salvation and the salvation of others.

There are times in which many of us are guilty of forgetting, or at least being a little blasé, about the wonders of our deliverance from the slavery and penalty of sin and the exceeding great riches of our inheritance in Christ.

An Iranian woman, when asked if she regretted all the persecution the Gospel had brought her, replied, "I would go through a hundred times as much trouble willingly for the joy that is in my heart; there was no joy before."

In his remarkable poem *The Everlasting Mercy*, John Mansfield tells the story of Saul Kane, a drunken, blaspheming, prize fighter who came to Christ through the witness of a godly Quaker woman. So changed was he, so much had he repented, and put his trust in the Saviour, that when he came out of the drinking house, his whole outlook on life was transformed and he exclaimed…

O glory of the lighted mind.
How dead I'd been, how dumb, how blind.
The station brook, to my new eyes,
Was babbling out of Paradise.
The waters rushing from the rain
Were singing Christ has risen again.
I thought all earthly creatures knelt
From rapture of the joy I felt.
The narrow station-wall's brick ledge,
The wild hop withering in the hedge,

Contagious Joy

The lights in huntsman's upper storey
Were parts of an eternal glory,
Were God's eternal garden flowers,
I stood in bliss at this for hours.

There is such a joy in trusting Jesus, and so many hymns and Christian songs recount that joy, and so does nature itself.

CH Spurgeon writes,

> When sin is pardoned, our greatest sorrow is ended, and our truest pleasure begins. Such is the joy which the Lord bestows upon His reconciled ones, that it overflows and fills all nature with delight. The material world has latent music in it, and a renewed heart knows how to bring it out and make it vocal.

Isaiah reports,

> *The mountains and the hills shall break forth into singing, and all the trees of the field shall clap their hands.*
>
> *Isaiah 55:12*

My wife and I are blessed in that we live just off the Chiltern Hills; in five minutes we can be on those open hills and everywhere the skylarks are nearly bursting their little blood vessels with their song. A group of skylarks have a very special unique name, "an exaltation." What a name! It always feels that those skylarks are reflecting our joy of knowing that the barriers are broken and we have access to the Father and are now hid with Christ in God.

Psalm 126:2 describes the joy of the exiled Jews returning to Jerusalem after their captivity in foreign lands, it was like a dream to them, *"then our mouth was filled with laughter, and our tongue with singing"*. When God, in His amazing grace, sets you free from your past captivity there is every reason to laugh, dance and sing.

A clean heart is a happy heart. Maybe for some, it is time to go back to those wells of salvation!

Joy is a net of love by which you can catch souls. A joyful heart is the inevitable result of a heart burning with love.

Mother Theresa

6

The Joy of Soul Winning

Those who are wise shall shine like the brightness of the firmament and those who turn many to righteousness, like the stars forever and ever.

Daniel 12:3

The joy of salvation is one thing, the joy of partnering with the Holy Spirit in leading someone into the place of faith and complete trust in Christ, is another immense joy to experience.

In October 1899, Mafeking in North West South Africa was besieged by the Boers. Two thousand British soldiers led by Baden Powell were surrounded by five thousand Boers. The siege would never have been so famous if it were not for the media, four newspaper reporters from London papers were trapped in the siege, and so the event was reported on every day in the papers. And what made the siege even more newsworthy was that amongst the besieged was the son of the Prime Minister and Sarah Wilson, daughter of the Duke of Marlborough who later became the aunt of Sir Winston Churchill.

The siege lasted seven months and the situation became desperate with everyone starving, but eventually a force of a thousand Cavalry along with some field guns broke through.

Contagious Joy

It was a time of great rejoicing for the inhabitants of Mafeking. The brave soldiers were mobbed by the crowds singing *Rule Britannia.* In London, the news was received with hysterical rejoicing. Crowds sang, danced in the streets and shouted themselves hoarse for hours.

In the light of all the great battles fought by the British, Mafeking was not of huge significance and, compared to saving a soul out of darkness into His glorious light, it fades into insignificance. The angel of the Lord announced to the shepherds, *"I bring you tidings of great joy," Luke 2:8.*

The gloriously great privilege of partnering with the Holy Spirit in leading a soul into the Kingdom, is really something to shout yourself hoarse about! Ask anyone who has had the joy of leading someone in a prayer of repentance and faith in Christ's finished work, and they will tell you.

Telling the Gospel story to those who have not committed themselves to the love of God is an immense joy. William Tyndale, who was the first to translate the scriptures for us into English, and was burnt at the stake for his trouble in 1536, opens up for us the word that is translated into the English as 'gospel'. Tyndale puts it this way.

> *'Evangelio'* is a Greek word, and signifies good, merry, glad and joyful tidings, that make a man's heart glad and make him sing, dance and leap for joy.

It has often been said, one joy we can only experience this side of heaven is to lead a soul, with the help of the Holy Spirit, out of darkness into His glorious light. I am sure that is true, but maybe we will enjoy even more in heaven, the reality of the small part we might have played in leading someone to Christ. Luke 15:7 tells us that there is great joy in heaven over one sinner who repents, so on this earth we can join with heaven's rejoicing.

Most readers will have not even been a twinkle in their father's eye when Billy Graham held his great evangelistic meetings in the UK in the 1950s. Thousands of lives were radically changed through those great meetings. Such joy spread through the churches as congregations witnessed the transformation in the lives of their families and friends that they had invited to the Billy Graham Crusades.

Read the histories of men like George Whitfield and John and Charles Wesley as they preached the message of "New Birth" across the UK and the America's, the joy comes bubbling through the pages.

Perhaps you have had the experience of someone introducing themselves to you, usually someone you do not recognise, and hear them saying, "You may not remember me, but twenty years ago you challenged me about Jesus' claims upon my life, and here I am today rejoicing in the goodness of God, having served the Lord all these years because you bothered to speak to me." What a joy! When we get to heaven and all things are revealed, I wonder what amazing, delightful surprises we shall enjoy.

In a later chapter we look at the joy of giving; however, there cannot be a greater gift anybody can ever give than to lead a person to Jesus, that they might have the amazing free gift of eternal life.

Christians ought to be celebrating constantly. We ought to be preoccupied with parties, banquets, feasts and merriment. We ought to give ourselves over to veritable orgies of joy, because we have been liberated from the fear of life and the fear of death. We ought to attract people to church quite literally by the fun there is in being a Christian.

Robert Hotchkins

7

The Joy of True Praise and Worship

> *Triumphant now, I'll bring him my offerings of praise, singing and shouting with ecstatic joy!*
>
> *Psalm 27:6 tPt.*

Jewish people have a long heritage of joyful festiveness in their coming together that shines through so strongly in the Scripture, especially the Psalms. As one looks at Psalms 149 and 150 you cannot help but see some of that exuberance. One rabbinical scholar tried to unwrap the meaning behind the word *"Hallelujah"* this way:

> "To shine – a brilliant, radiant, conspicuous shininess that can't be ignored. Make a show of celebrating with boasting and continuous, noisy foolish-sounding raving."

We might see that kind of behaviour in a football match, but not often in a church celebration, more is the pity.

Surely worship and enjoyment go together, for we are expressing our joy and delight in the Lord when we worship and praise Him. When the referee blows the whistle at the end of a football match and one side has made a resounding victory, what delight and joy is expressed by the winning side's supporters; they go wild with joy, hugging one another and shouting themselves hoarse, giving their praises to their wonderful team. That is why football supporters travel sometimes hundreds of miles, even halfway across the world, spending huge sums of money to attend football matches to enjoy and rejoice in their team. One notices that this rejoicing is very much a corporate activity, half the enjoyment is the shared experience.

A joy shared is multiplied, and so when we come together with others to worship, there is a multiplication of joy. That is why football enthusiasts, when they cannot attend a match, much prefer to watch the game with others on the TV in a pub or club rather than on their own at home.

Some of the most ecstatic, joyous, fulfilling experiences I have ever known have been found when I have been in worship to the Lord in the great congregation. There have been times, even in old age when my knees don't really like it or appreciate it, when I have leapt and danced for joy. Mary sings in the Magnificat, as she shares her pregnancy with her cousin Elizabeth,

> *My soul is ecstatic, overflowing with praises to God! My spirit bursts with joy over my life-giving God.*
>
> *Luke 1:46 tPt.*

I believe many would express the same experience. More often than not, the word "joy" or "joyful" in scripture is related to worship, and for so many, our happiest moments in life have been in corporate worship.

I must be honest and say that there have been times in congregational worship, (may the Good Lord forgive me!) when "joy" is not a word that comes immediately to mind. "Boring", would be more appropriate, or thoughts like, "Will the worship leader stop wittering on so, that we can worship the Lord." There have been moments in my experience when the worship leading from the front by singers and musicians was such an excruciating cacophony, that I would have rather laid on the floor and done press ups. But when in the company of a group of like-minded Christians who are passionate about Jesus and love to extol Him, it is so easy to know great joy in worship.

People become like the God they worship!

Paul writes,

> *We all with unveiled face, beholding as in a mirror the glory of the Lord, are being transformed into the same image from glory to glory.*
>
> *2 Corinthians 3:18*

The more we gaze on Jesus, the more like Him we become. The Psalms speak of how Israel worshiped idols and became like the idols they worshiped,

> *...they became useless like the God's they worshipped.*
>
> *Psalm 135:18*

Ancient Egyptians worshipped animals, and history tells us they became like the animals they worshipped. If our concept of God is one of stoicism and lacking in emotion, then we also will begin to become stoic and unemotional. If we see our Father in Heaven as one who is filled with exuberant joy, we also will be joyful. We reflect the God we worship.

Practising the "Presence", seems to be the key. Brother Lawrence, the seventeenth century Carmelite monk, who cultivated the lifestyle of living in the presence of God in every facet and action in life, learnt to practise the Presence of God, and experienced as a result such an unrestrained joy, and said,

> The goal which we must set before ourselves is to be in this life the most perfect worshippers of God possible, as one would hope to be through eternity.

In the introduction of Jack Hayford's book *Manifest Presence*, Hayford speaks of a renewal of worship going on in the church. He asks, "What is this worship awakening about?"

> It isn't about the music.
>
> It isn't about becoming 'contemporary'.
>
> It isn't about cultural awareness.
>
> It isn't about being 'cool,' 'hip' or 'with it'.
>
> It isn't about misty-eyed intimacy with God.
>
> It isn't about theological accuracy about God. But…
>
> It's about the formation of hearts in the presence of God.
>
> It's about the shaping of disciples who know Him through being with Him.
>
> It is about the transforming work the Holy Spirit achieves when pure worship occurs.
>
> And it's preparation for the last battle.

We could spend a great deal of time and energy defining worship, but to my mind it is basically an expression of our relationship with the Trinity. Something that is at the same time simple and yet complex.

At our wedding service, if some of us can remember that far back, we vowed to our partners, "With my body I thee worship." What joy was ours as husband and wife gave themselves completely to one another. The joy of giving ourselves completely to God by worshipping *"in spirit and in truth"* can be even more transcending. We can discover our entire human person being enriched in His presence.

Jack Hayford describes worship this way,

> Full-absorbed worship, then, is not just spiritual and from the heart; neither is it just a cerebral pursuit, a mystical consciousness or emotional binge. But in the light of God's Word, worship is about the presentation of our total being – that is body, mind, emotions and spirit – ignited by the Holy Spirit as a living sacrifice.

Hayford goes on to say in his book that we worship Him,

1. With our regenerated spirits;
2. With our renewed minds;
3. With our revived emotions; and
4. With our rededicated bodies."

The Apostle Paul must have experienced this sublime experience, that is why he urged the church in Romans,

> *I beseech you therefore brethren, by the mercies of God, to present your bodies a living sacrifice, holy, acceptable to God, which is your reasonable sacrifice.*
>
> *Romans 12:1.*

Something happens when we worship, it determines outcomes, it most certainly "rolls out the red carpet" for the King of Joy to come into our midst.

One of the great things about worship is that the entire focus is on the Lord. If I were to spend too long looking inward at myself and my own inadequacies, I would soon become very depressed. Be introspective long enough, and I would have a mental breakdown. What a joy to focus on Him who is so glorious, awesome, perfect and loving.

Contagious Joy

I understand that paediatric specialists have discovered that the joy centre of a baby's brain is activated and develops through looking into the adoring, smiling faces of its parents. That is why we need a face to face encounter with our Heavenly Dad. Perhaps the reason some find so little joy in worship, and have never learnt how to enjoy the Lord, is because they have never allowed God to minister to their hearts and let Him love them; they have never seen His smiling face gazing adoringly at them so that their facility for joy in worship has never been activated and developed.

8

The Joy of Trust

When I fully trust in you, help is on the way.
I jump for joy and burst forth with ecstatic,
passionate praise!

Psalm 28:7 tPt

Your victory heaps blessing after blessing upon him. What joy and bliss he tastes, rejoicing before your face! For the king ***trusts endlessly in you,*** *and he will never stumble, never fall.*

Psalm 21:6-7 tPt

The Apostle Peter says,

> *Through believing in Him you are saturated with an ecstatic joy...for you are reaping the harvest of your faith.*
>
> *1 Peter1:8-9 tPt*

There is such joy in simple trust; when you know that you know that Father God has everything under control and has your best interests at heart, there comes a harvest of joy.

Doubt and unbelief bring distress, but when we trust the Lord even when we are sad, in due season our faith works its work and we find ourselves rejoicing in the Lord. Who of us, has not known times of sadness, perhaps at a loved one or someone close whose lack of love for the Lord has caused grief of mind? Yet as you have turned your eyes on the Lord and put your trust in His Holy Name, Jehovah-Nissi, you know that He will conquer every foe and you begin to rejoice.

Personally, I have known much turmoil of mind and spirit before I have made up my mind on an issue to trust God, but once I've stepped over the line and made a decision, the joy has come. When over twenty years ago Vanessa and I resigned our salaried roles in ministry and stepped out trusting that God would supply all our needs, with no secure form of income, what a great joy and adventure it has been as month after month, year after year, God has miraculously supplied all our needs and then some, sometimes from such unexpected quarters.

Trusting Jesus brings so much joy as it sets you free from so much worry and fret. No wonder John Wesley once said, "I would no more fret than swear." From my earliest Christian experience He has always rewarded every little step of faith I have ever taken, from my decision to enter Bible College at the age of twenty two years and only twenty months old as a born again believer, to asking Vanessa if she would go out with me. From preaching for the very first time to the youth group in Ilford Elim Church sixty-three years ago, to prophesying to a congregation of over 6,000 in Brazil. No wonder the psalmist could sing,

> *But let all those rejoice who put their trust in You; let them ever* ***shout for joy****, because You defend them; let all those who love Your name be joyful in You. Psalm 5:11 NKJ*

Joy does not have to be linked to circumstances; it so often comes as a result of trusting the Lord. As I mentioned earlier in the book, we remember the fantastic praises of Israel in Exodus 15, when God so miraculously rescued them from the

Egyptians and brought them through the Red Sea. They were so happy, as they sang,

> *He has triumphed gloriously! The horse and the rider He has thrown into the sea.*
>
> *Exodus 15:1*

At that moment, they were rejoicing in their changed circumstances. Prior to the crossing they were scared out of their wits and wished they were back in the slavery of Egypt. It was not a pretty picture. Their joy in Exodus 15 was not wrong, it is always so important to celebrate your victories, but here was the problem, they had the right song, but the wrong side of the Red Sea. Israel, instead of moaning at Moses, should have trusted the Lord and praised Him for His deliverance **before** they crossed over.

Paul prays,

> *Now, may the God of hope fill you with **all joy** and peace in **believing.***
>
> *Romans 15:13*

The apostle uses the word "filled" with joy; I guess that means we could be half-filled or quarter-filled. Maybe the level of our faith is almost a spiritual "dip-stick" to measure our joy level! He certainly says that this joy is the result of believing, and he also prefaces his statement with *"now";* whatever our circumstances, as we trust Him the joy rises.

There are many verses that encourage us to offer up the sacrifice of praise. **A great key in life is to intentionally by faith stir up joy, before we see the victory.** That is why the writer to the Hebrews writes,

Contagious Joy

> *Therefore by Him let us continually offer the sacrifices of praise to God, that is, the fruit of our lips, giving thanks to His name.*
>
> *Hebrews 12:15*

Prior to the verse the writer is speaking of future blessings, so obviously he is referring to blessings yet to come. The psalmist expresses the same thought,

> *Let them sacrifice the sacrifice of thanksgiving, and declare His works with rejoicing.*
>
> *Psalm 107:22*

Even CH Spurgeon, the Prince of Preachers, no Pentecostal, over 150 years ago knew what it was to laugh for the sheer joy of believing what the Lord has said will be accomplished. On one occasion writing,

> This is a precious word from our Lord's own lips. It has made the writer laugh for joy.

Everyone loves the poetry of Psalm 23, so many in Christendom can recite it by heart, but how many know the joy of when you know beyond all doubt, that God is your Fierce Protector and Pastor who generously provides for your every need? Who chases after you with His goodness? The psalmist is singing about a life without lack in which one is completely satisfied and sustained, **no matter what happens.**

On my wife Pamela's tombstone is written, "She gave her all and touched the lives of so many." That statement summed up her life, she gave herself to others, so much so, that her school where she worked as a teacher, closed for the afternoon so that staff and pupils could attend her funeral. How many of us could it be written on our tombstones, "The Lord was his/her shepherd and he/she never lacked."?
Dallas Willard defined joy this way,

The Joy of Trust

> Joy is a pervasive sense of well-being that claims your entire body and soul, both physical and the nonphysical side of the human self.

Joy comes naturally when we have great confidence, acting with faith in The Good Shepherd, and we have faith in who we are in Him and what we are doing with Him.

My life verse is found in 2 Timothy 2:1. God has blessed me with a special revelation about this verse,

> *My son, stand strong in the* **grace** *that is in Christ Jesus.*

For over sixty years that verse has reminded me that no matter what the challenge, situation or circumstance, His grace is more than enough. As I have exercised my faith in that promise, not only has it nerved me to go forward, there has also been a joy of absolute trust in the extravagant, undeserved mercies of God.

A similar verse has also become another life verse – 2 Corinthians 9:8. Reader, do you want an injection of joy? Get hold of this verse and believe it!

> *And God is able to make all* ***grace*** *abound towards you, that you always having all sufficiency in all things, may have an abundance for every good work.*

The Apostle Paul could say to the Philippians,

> ***Rejoice in the Lord always. Again I say rejoice!***

I noticed how the humblest and at the same time the most balanced and capacious minds, praised most, whilst the cranks, misfits and malcontents praised least.

CS Lewis
Reflections on the Psalms

9

The Joy of Service

Make a joyful shout to the Lord, all you lands! Serve the Lord with gladness; come before His presence with singing.

Psalm 100:1-2

The psalmist is exhorting us to live a life of celebration and joy in serving the Lord, like King David who endeavoured to do all that his hands found to do, as to the Lord. Steve Buckland notes in his book *Possessing Joy,*

> Whenever we consistently relinquish joy in an assignment from God, we have most likely hit the ceiling of our ministry influence. Our gladness level is one indicator of whether we are ready for greater responsibilities and callings.

Chuck Swindoll writes,

> I refuse to force hilarity into the back seat every time responsibility takes the wheel. If the fun's gone, it's because we did not want it around – not because it did not fit…I don't care if your "to do" list is as long as the horizon, you need to get back into balance and take time to laugh…dance… and to love. Why? Because the Bible says so! Furthermore, your family and friends will enjoy you a lot more when you do.

I love Dr Brian Simmonds translation of Ephesians 5:16,

> *Take full advantage of every day as you spend your life for His purposes. tPt*

I am so challenged by those words that I have written them on the front cover of my journal to remind me every day that my joyful work is to do His will. There have been other such reminders that at different seasons I have used to stimulate my focus for the day. In John Ortberg's book, *Soul Keeping* he quotes his mentor Dallas Willard,

> You must arrange your days so that you are experiencing deep contentment, **joy,** and confidence in your everyday life with God.

I have copied this quote in the front of my Bible to remind me how to arrange my life!

The first phrase, like those above, that I ever used to encourage myself was, ***"Everything joyfully for His Glory."*** At one stage I had those words stuck to my shaving mirror. Surely, this is how to live – joyfully serving Him!

You do meet those who love to remind you of all the good things they do, all the sacrifices they make. As we know, *"they have their reward"!*

Jesus said,

> *When you have done all those things that were commanded say...We have done what was our duty.*
>
> *Luke 17:10.*

We all deserve recognition for the good we do, and we all thrive on appreciation, but many times we do not receive any thanks. When that happens, we can react three different ways:

1. We can give in to self-pity and go around the world complaining of how life is not fair.
2. We can give way to resentment and develop a great chip on our shoulder and wonder why everyone gives us a wide berth.
3. We can adopt the attitude Jesus taught and say, "I'm only doing what God expects of me. And knowing He is pleased with me is reward enough."

If we try to run on the fuel of other people's encouragement and praise, when that praise does not come, you'll have no joy. The *"joy of the Lord"* comes from knowing you live under the smile of His approval. There is no joy like knowing that you are doing what God has asked you to do. There really is joy in serving Jesus.

CH Spurgeon, in his devotional book *Cheque Book of the Bank of Faith*, gives a devotional thought on

> *In that day HOLINESS UNTO THE LORD shall be engraved on the bells of the horses.*
>
> *Zechariah 14:20*

Spurgeon says,

> Happy day when all things shall be consecrated, and the horse's bells shall ring out, holiness to the Lord.

Horses in Spurgeon's day were rarely related to pleasure as they are today; they were objects that spoke of labour, toil and hard work. Spurgeon implies that "labour and toil" when given as service to Jesus can be a joyful experience,

> From morning to evening I would order all things by a happy and holy rule – why should they not? Even my horses shall have bells – who has such a right to music as the saints have? But all my bells, my music, my mirth, shall be turned to

holiness, and shall ring out the name of 'The Happy God.'

Is there a greater joy in labour than when that labour is an act of worship to Him?

Anyone who is knowledgeable of the history of furniture making will know of "Shaker" furniture. To this day manufacturers endeavour to copy "Shaker" furniture or reproduce "Shaker" style furniture. Shakers were a breakaway sect of the Quakers, founded in 1747, they died out as a denomination possibly over 100 years ago. The Shakers were so called because of their practice of shaking, dancing, shouting, and speaking in tongues. Shakers believed that work should be an act of worship to the Lord and so they made furniture as an act of worship and therefore their work was functional, but as strong and perfect as they could possibly make it, hence such furniture is valued to this day. They also invented many useful tools that are still in use today like the circular saw. What a joyful thought that our work bench or work desk, our serving counter, can be a place of worship! As you go to work on Monday morning, don't let anything or anyone stop you enjoying it!

Many in these days, work from home, which offers us another great excuse to make our homes places of joyous worship. Our homes are our base of operation from which we can work for the Lord and also launch out into the world around us.

Abraham, the Father of our faith, set us a wonderful example in that whenever he had an encounter with God or wherever he settled in Canaan, he set up an altar, a focus for his worship of Jehovah. We too need to set up altars in our homes (I am not suggesting you set up a special table or shelf with a cross and candles etc., although if that helps...) to make them places of worship and intercession, Houses of Prayer. The promise is,

The Joy of Service

I will make them joyful in the house of prayer.
Isaiah 56:7

Prayer is work for the Lord, but it can be joyful work.

The great Evangelist of the early twentieth century, Gypsy Smith, said,

> When the great end of the day comes, the greatest joy of all will be the joy of knowing you have tried to make somebody else's life happy.

I know that it always gives me "a real shot in the arm" when I know I have caused a bit of happiness in this miserable old world. It gives me great joy when folks write me a line and say how blessed and encouraged they have been through something I have written in one of my books, or a sermon I preached. The last few years I have posted a Bulletin, sometimes twice a month with a few of my ruminations and leadership tips, plus a few jokes. Every month people respond and some say how they have been encouraged or inspired, which is a great encouragement to me and gives me joy, but if I am ever aware that God is happy with me over something I have done for Him, I feel delirious.

Brother Lawrence, who we mention in an earlier chapter, made it a principle of life to do everything, whether it be washing dishes, to prayer in the chapel, to do it as an act of love to God. This led to…

> …his soul revelling in joys so unbroken and so strong that sometimes, to control them and prevent their being outwardly visible, he was constrained to manifest juvenile behaviour which smacked rather of folly than devotion.

If we could follow his example what happy people we would be!

The Old Testament prophets, Haggai and Zechariah, were commissioned to encourage the remnant of Israel that had returned to Jerusalem to rebuild the temple. It was where God wanted His people to focus their efforts at that time. Haggai prophesied for just three and a half months and his message was simple, "If you will get on and work on the project God has given you, God has promised to be with you." We know as believers, we can do nothing of worth in Kingdom terms without God's blessing and presence, but to hear God say, ***"I am with you!"*** in a project and to have evidence of that in some tangible way, brings special joy. As the old hymn goes, "There is joy, joy, joy in serving Jesus."

Those that only serve their own ends, that have a hidden agenda to all that they do, haven't a clue as to the joy and the wonder that they are missing.

Deuteronomy 28 tells us of the incredible blessings that would come to Israel if they were obedient and kept God's laws, also all the curses that would come upon them if they were disobedient. One of the reasons for the curses of God to come crashing down upon their heads was,

> *Because you did not serve the Lord your God with* ***joy and gladness of heart****, for the abundance of everything.*
>
> *Deuteronomy 28:47*

As an early church father wrote,

> **He is not holy who is not happy.**

10

The Joy of Giving

Mean people find it hard to be cheerful.
Archbishop Sentamu

God loves a cheerful giver.
2 Corinthians 9:7

If God says that He loves something, it is a moment to tune in and listen. Of course, God loves everybody, but there is something that especially moves His heart when someone gives joyously. There are seven things in the Bible that God loves:

- The resident foreigner or immigrant (Deuteronomy 10:19),
- Righteousness in our affairs with others (Psalm 11:7),
- Justice (Psalm 37:28),
- The gates of Zion (Psalm 87:2),
- His righteous people (Psalm 146:8),
- Those He disciplines (Hebrews 12:6),
- And a hilarious giver (2 Corinthians 9:7).

I think the reason God enjoys our cheerful giving is because it is so in line with His heart, as He delights in mercy. True love is always a self-giving act. Who does not enjoy a gift from a friend or loved one all the more when it is given to you joyfully? I love it when I visit congregations who burst into praise, clapping and cheering as the offering is announced. Surely, it is a moment to jump for joy, certainly not to be grudgingly morose or unhappy.

The Greek word for cheerful is *hilaros.* The earliest known hymn outside the Bible that is still in use to this very day, some using it every evening, in the Orthodox, Armenian, Anglican and Lutheran churches, is called *A Hymn to the Hilarious Light*. What a beautiful title! It is one thing to give joyfully and hopefully, but there is something radical about giving hilariously, for it truly is,

> *More blessed to give than to receive.*
>
> *Acts 20:35*

May our hearts join with the heart of the *Hilarious Light.*

The writer to the Hebrews tells us *to provoke one another to love and good works,* therefore, we should make it our joy to encourage and provoke one another to give, by our teaching and example; as Henry Rosso says,

> Fund raising is the gentle art of teaching the joy of giving.

When I was a young and immature Pastor, I found great difficulty teaching in the church on the subject of giving. I had experienced some difficult situations arising out of the negative culture of the British when it comes to the subject of money. I remember one person becoming so upset and leaving the church because I suggested they might like to take a Missionary Box. The person felt that all I wanted was her money! Asking for money can somehow "get up the nose" of some, especially people who possess a poverty spirit. As I have grown older and uglier, I have come to realise that encouraging people to give is encouraging them into a joyous blessing and there is no way that I will now apologise for asking people to give to a worthy cause. Fund raising really is a way to make people happy.

The ability to give joyfully is a grace given by God. The Apostle Paul speaks about,

> *...grace filled generosity.*
> *2 Corinthians 8:1-7*

I love the way Dr Brian Simmons in his *Passion* translation writes this passage about the churches in Macedonia,

> *For even during a season of severe difficulty and tremendous suffering, they became* ***even more filled with joy.*** *From the depths of their extreme poverty,* ***super-abundant joy*** *overflowed into an act of extravagant generosity.*

There is a real grace from God in giving joyfully, also in receiving joyfully. The grace of receiving is even more rare than the grace of giving, but how important it is for us to learn how to receive well, because when we do, we can enhance the joy of the giver. A quote I wrote down in the past has remained with me,

> Receive joyfully, if you want people to give joyfully.

It does take faith to give well, to believe that your giving is pleasing to Him and to believe that as you give, it will be given unto you, (although not necessarily in kind). Vanessa and I have been on a journey concerning our giving. As we have given, God has miraculously met our needs and as our faith has grown, so we have learnt to increase the percentage of our giving. It has been such fun as God has surprised and delighted us with His unexpected ways of meeting our needs.

There is a very special joy in giving when you give out of your own need. There have been times when Vanessa and I having found ourselves seriously challenged financially with bills looming that we did not have the necessary funds to cover, we would give out of our poverty like the Macedonians, and then find God stepping in with His largess. It really is more blessed to give than to receive.

11

The Joy of Fellowship

So continuing daily with one accord in the Temple, and breaking bread from house to house, they ate their food with gladness and simplicity of heart, praising God and having...
Acts 2:46,47

We find immense joy in our relationship with the Holy Trinity, but as Mark Twain said, that joy is much increased when we can share it with others.

Writing this book in the midst of a "lockdown" during the Covid-19 pandemic, the greatest feelings of loss for most active Christians is the act of corporate worship, and the living fellowship and friendship with brothers and sisters in Christ, which cannot be enjoyed to the same degree in a Zoom meeting on a computer screen. Being an extrovert, I feed on the fellowship of like-minded souls, I love and enjoy people, it is my bread and butter, it is my great joy.

God is not an isolationist, He is a Trinity, and He has made us in His own image to interact with others. From the beginning man was made for relationship with God and with his fellow man or woman, it was to be part of his joy and delight in life. Take away our relationship with others and we cannot function properly in the world or in the church.

To heal our relationship with the Father and with one another was the whole purpose of Christ's great sacrifice.

The hymn *Blest Be The Tie That Binds*, was written by Dr John Fawcett. John was the pastor of a very poor Baptist congregation in Yorkshire. His salary was £25 per year, which was totally inadequate, so he accepted a call to a very large influential church in London. He preached his farewell sermon and was loading his belongings onto wagons for removal to London, when sorrowing members of his congregation, showing deep affection and grief, pleaded with him not to leave them. John and his wife were so overcome they sat down and wept. "Oh John, John, I can't bear this," said his poor wife. "We shall not go," said the good man. This decision was hailed with great joy by his people. So, Dr Fawcett wrote the hymn to commemorate that the loving fellowship of the saints was worth far more than money or physical comfort.

It is understood that fellowship with other saints is not always sweet. CH Spurgeon said that he would rather spend time with some in heaven than spend half an hour with them on earth. But fellowship of kindred hearts is one of the great joys of life.

As a gardener, I know when plants are happy, it is when they are in vigorous growth, producing flowers and fruit and that usually does not happen without **loving care**. Human beings are no different to plants in that respect, we are much happier when we are expanding our capabilities or increasing our skills, growing in our understanding and especially when we grow more like Him. Personal growth rarely happens without interaction with others, and without **loving care**. If we desire to be disciples of Jesus, that of necessity entails learning and living with others. One of the joys of Christian life is meeting up with a group of people of like mind and heart who stimulate and challenge you, cause you to stretch your faith, and also love each other. Jesus said,

> *By this all will know that you are My disciples, if you have love for one another. John 13:35*

Meet with a group of people who do not demonstrate their love for you and do not stimulate you, and you will soon get bored, because the meeting is no fun.

The reason some churches fail and die, or Life Groups collapse is because the fellowship is not sweet, real or stimulating; they are not a happy, joyful experience.

Grief can take care of itself,
but to get the full value of joy, we must
have somebody to divide it with.
Mark Twain

12

The Joy of Tribulation

In the world you will have tribulation; but be of good cheer, I have overcome the world.
John 16:33

My brethren, count it all joy when you fall into various trials.
James 1:2

I found this chapter the most challenging to write. I ask myself, "How can we ever rejoice in trouble, for even if you run from it, or do your best to avoid it, trouble will find you; and what about persecution? How can one rejoice in suffering for Christ?"

We know that trials can strengthen our faith and purify us; most of us must admit we have become bigger and better people because of the tests and dark times that we have endured. The psalmist sings,

> *It is good for me that I have been afflicted, that I may learn Your statutes.*
> *Psalm 119:71*

Job speaks of,

> *...coming forth as pure gold.*
> *Job 23:10*

Yet, when early believers were being persecuted for Christ sake, they somehow found the persecution a delight! In Acts we read,

> *When they had called for the apostles and beaten them, they commanded that they should not speak in the name of Jesus, and let them go. So they departed from the presence of the council, **rejoicing** that they were counted worthy to suffer shame for His name.*

Again in Acts we witness Paul and Silas in the dark dungeon of a Philippian jail with their backs torn open by whips and chained to a wall, they could sing songs of joy to the Lord because they were suffering for Jesus. James writes,

> *My fellow believers, when it seems as though you are facing nothing but difficulties see it as an invaluable opportunity to experience **the greatest joy you can**.*
>
> *James 1:2 tPt*

The NKJ Bible translates the verse ***"My brethren count it all joy".*** It is significant that James uses the word *"count"*. James was called by the early church "James the Just", because he was such an upright man. Tradition has it that James, being such a trustworthy man, kept the books for the fishing business in Galilee. So James uses an accounting word "count". I believe what James is trying to tell us is that life has its profits and losses and when you add up all of life's experiences, suffering does a great deal for your character, it is God's loving plan that all that negativity that life throws at you, all the "slings and arrows", can work out for our good, it can be profit all the way to the bank of heaven.

So, when bad things happen, we have some choices to make. We can consider life unfair, unjust and complain bitterly. We can consider negative experiences as the judgement of God and spiral into despair. We can see it as a chance to demonstrate our resilience and strength in adversity. We can become angry and seek revenge, or we can simply be overcome by the sadness. But James exhorts, rejoice because there are some great outcomes, you are going to be a better person, you are going to shine more brightly once the gold has gone through the furnace. It is all working for your good!

After Job's utter loss of everything that he held dear, Bildad says to him,

> *He will yet fill your mouth with laughing, and your lips with rejoicing.*
>
> *Job 8:21*

Habakkuk gives us some wonderful insight when he prophesies to the nation of Judah just before its annihilation by the Babylonians, pleading with them to repent before the judgement of God crashes down on them, but to no avail. The vision of Judah's impending destruction nearly destroys his sensitive soul,

> *My body trembled; my lips quivered at the voice; rottenness entered my bones and I trembled in myself.*
>
> *Habakkuk 3:16*

The pain of what was about to happen could have destroyed him, but he continues,

> *Yet I will rejoice in the Lord, I will joy in the God of my salvation.*

He made a decision of his will to keep his eyes on God in the midst of all the pain, and believe that God was still in control in spite of the evidence that seemed to say otherwise.

One of the most amazing examples of this was Corrie Ten Boom's story of her harrowing experiences during World

War II in a Nazi concentration camp, with death, depravity, and day after day, human cruelty on a monumental scale all around her. Corrie had to watch her sister being destroyed by the privations and eventually die, and yet she never lost sight of her Lord and Master who gave her strength to endure and live to tell her story. Terrible, unimaginable suffering can not only be endured, but triumphed over by looking up to Him.

That is why Jesus said,

> *In the world you will have tribulation: but be of good cheer, I have overcome the world.*
>
> *John 6:33*

In this world trouble is inevitable; as CH Spurgeon says,

> The flail is not hung up out of the way, nor can I hope that it will be laid aside so long as I lie on the threshing floor. This world is not our home. This is the place of the furnace, and the forge, and the hammer. But what is the Lord's argument that He uses to encourage us? *I have overcome the world.* We need to see that the enemy has already been overcome. We fight a defeated foe. We can "cheer up", when we look to our victorious Lord, the world has already been conquered. Hallelujah!

Jesus said that when we are persecuted because of Him, we should,

> ***Rejoice and leap for joy***. *Blessed are you when men hate you, and when they exclude you, and revile you, and cast out your name as evil, for the Son of Man's sake. Rejoice in that day and leap for joy! For indeed your reward is great in heaven.*
>
> *Luke 6:23*

Jesus is telling us that when things are tough, **intentionally stir up joy.** Like King David, when everything was stacked against him, he encouraged himself in the Lord (1 Samuel 30:6). Jesus said, ***"Rejoice in that day".*** On the day it happens, at that moment, in that same hour, make a decision and then ***leap for joy!*** When people have it in for you, the last thing you feel like doing is to leap for joy, but there is a great secret here. Doing something physical can break the spirit of heaviness. The temptation when we are under great pressure and loss is to sit in the corner, do nothing and feel sorry for yourself, like Elijah under the Juniper tree, but what we should do is get up and physically leap, just as Elijah was commanded by God to get up and get on with the work in hand.

When I first started my relationship with Jesus at the age of 19 years, I was handed a *Navigators* course for new believers with a little wallet full of memory cards with verses of scripture printed on them. Those first memory verses have stood me in great stead for over 65 years. One particular verse that has been of the greatest help over those years was,

> *No temptation has overtaken you except such as is common to man; but God is faithful, who will not allow you to be tempted beyond what you are able, but with the temptation will also make the way of escape, that you may be able to bare it.*
> *1 Corinthians 10:13*

For me, it was a long verse to memorise, but what a saving, releasing, encouraging word it has been to me.

The Lord has far more faith in us that we have in Him; if He allows some great challenge to come our way, it means that Father believes we have what it takes to face the challenge. He would not allow (suffer) you to be tempted beyond your capabilities to cope; with the challenge He gives the grace.

No one in Christ can say, “This too much!”, “I cannot go on.”, “I cannot cope with this pressure.” If Father God has permitted it, it means that His grace is sufficient for you to rise above it, and not let it destroy you. ***He will not allow you to be tempted above what you are able.*** He always makes a way for you to escape.

Sometimes we just have to hold the tension of not knowing or understanding what is going on in our lives and still trusting Him. As William Cowper writes in his great hymn, *God Moves In a Mysterious Way*,

Judge not the Lord by feeble sense,
But trust Him for His grace;
Behind a frowning providence
He hides a smiling face.

His purposes will ripen fast,
Unfolding every hour;
The bud may have a bitter taste,
But sweet will be the flower.

So, we can rejoice and,

In everything give thanks.
1 Thessalonians 5:18

Handel wrote the entire *Messiah* in just three weeks. He said the music came out of him in a flurry of notes and motifs. He seemed to be driven by an unseen hand to put pen to paper. Yet he wrote when his eyesight was failing and was facing the threat of a lingering death in debtors’ prison because of all his outstanding bills that he could not pay.

Most people would find it almost impossible to be creative when under great stress with physical and financial pressures, and yet Handel wrote a masterpiece under this terrible great cloud over his life. He declared that the secret was **“joy”**. He said, “He would burst with joy at what he was hearing in his mind and heart." We know that he lived to pay off all his debtors and raise great sums of money to help the poor and destitute.

The joy of the Lord is our strength. Heaven's joy destroys all the miseries of the enemy of our souls and sends him off with his tail between his legs.

True happiness is not attained through self-gratification, but through fidelity to a worthy purpose.

Helen Keller

13

The Joy of Discovery

My wife Pamela had a rather unique engagement ring, it was made by an uncle who worked in Hatton Garden, it consisted of three diamonds all cut from the same stone. Staying in a chalet attending a denominational conference, Pamela noticed that one of the diamonds was missing from her engagement ring. We hunted high and low especially outside the chalet on a gravel path where Pam had walked. It was like looking for a needle in a haystack. We searched for well over an hour, when suddenly Pam went into the bathroom and shook her towel in the bath and out dropped the diamond into the bath. It was a joy we never forgot. It was like Jesus' parables in Luke 15 of the woman who rejoiced in finding her lost coin, and the shepherd his lost sheep.

My present wife, Vanessa and I live in the Chiltern Hills and one of our great joys is to walk in the beautiful countryside that surrounds us. Our greatest joy is the fact that there is so much to discover, even after seventeen years of exploration, week after week we discover fresh vistas, new footpaths, new woods to explore, new flowers to identify, to be surprised by a deer, a fox, a hare or even a weasel.

It would seem God finds a special delight in hiding things from His children so that they can know the joy of discovery, like a treasure hunt or an Easter Egg hunt. Was this one of the reasons Jesus spoke in parables and often did not try to unwrap all the great statements He made, so that we could know the joy of seeking an answer for ourselves and knowing the joy of sudden revelation?

> *In that hour Jesus rejoiced in the Spirit and said, "I thank You, Father, Lord of heaven and earth, that You have hidden these things from the wise and prudent and revealed them to babes."*

The Word of God brings such joy in this way as we discover its deep "mind blowing" treasurers. The psalmist sings,

> *I rejoice at your word as one who finds great treasure.*
>
> *Psalm 119:162*

I recently received a long letter from a close friend, and he entitled his epistle, "The worst and best year of his life." In the letter he tells of how twelve months ago he was diagnosed with motor neurone disease. As we know, there is no known cure for this horrible disease and the physical deterioration for him has been rapid. Yet he wrote, "This is the most amazing year of my life." He has been a very active Christian for over fifty years, but his discoveries this year have been "enough to inspire and motivate for a life-time." So many things that, all the years of his Christian experience, were head knowledge, have become a daily experience. His understanding of "sonship", the kingdom of God, end times, and his understanding of "God being so much bigger and more loving than his previous image." He has felt a changed man by so many fresh revelations and discoveries that have made his heart dance for joy.

When, through the ministry of the Holy Spirit, we receive fresh revelation about His character, of our sonship, of how He answers prayer, of how He makes us more than conquerors, of how He lines up our destinies and inheritance, of how to exercise our faith in new ways, it brings us such overwhelming joy. Every day fresh discoveries. Surely this is the life He has chosen for us, not just now in time, but through eternity. In heaven we will, throughout eternity, discover fresh facets of His Glory. That is why the four living beasts in Revelation 4, before the throne of God, full of eyes, look on the glory of God and cry, *"Holy!"* It is as if they have never seen anything so amazing before and they look again and with fresh wonder of discovery, they cry yet again, *"Holy!"* And yet again they look…

Heaven is always new, we read in Revelation that it will be a New Jerusalem, and we shall have new names, we will sing a new song, and Jesus declares, ***"Behold I make all things new"***, *Revelation 21:5.* I think hell will be the same old thing, committing the same old self-destructive sins, whilst in heaven it will be continual glorious discovery. Here is another good reason to pray *Your will be done on earth as it is in heaven.*

The root of faith produces the flower of heart-joy.

CH Spurgeon

14

The Joy of Laughing With God

A time to weep. A time to laugh.
Ecclesiastes 3:4

As soldiers of Christ we have been equipped with many weapons of warfare and the battle is so fierce and violent we need use every weapon in the divine armoury:

The sword of the Spirit.
The shield of faith.
The breastplate of righteousness (weapons of righteousness on the right hand and the left, as Paul quotes to the church in Corinth).
The helmet of salvation.
The belt of truth.
The blood of Jesus.
The word of our testimony.
The shout of faith.
Lifting up holy hands.
Worship and praise.
The name of Jesus.
Taking communion.
And one often not recognised…Laughing with God.

Back in 2008 I developed a backache, and for the next two years I experienced a great deal of pain and misery. At times I found myself on powerful prescribed pain killers, moments when I could not even sit in the car, never mind drive it. There were nights when I could not sleep in bed unless I put myself in a special position with a cushion between my knees, and often, even that did not help, and found myself sleeping in an extending armchair downstairs where I could find a measure of comfort. Of course, I prayed and never stopped praying. I would ask churches to pray for me, people with a unique healing ministry to pray, anybody that I trusted, to pray. I went to physiotherapists who gave me daily exercises, chiropractors that made me feel worse. My GP said to me, "Brian, it is the wear and tear of old age. You will not always be in this much pain, it will come and go, but basically you will have to live with it, not much can be done."

One day I was reading Psalm 2 and read that the Lord sits in heaven listening to the plans of the rulers of this world and laughs. Inspired by the devil, the rulers of this world make plans and devise schemes that are contrary to the purposes of God. God just laughs at their dictates and plans, and holds them in derision.

The devil, as always, has a lot to say and many of us are far more tuned into his voice than God's. People fail to comprehend what a "past master" he is at spinning lies into seeming truths, and they are taken in by his "so called" truths. But whatever the devil says, it will always be inconsistent with the promises of God. The best thing we can do, when the devil speaks, is to take our place and sit with Christ in the heavenly realms, and have a good belly laugh with the Father. From experience I can say that responding to the devil's lies with laughter is a powerful liberating experience.

For three or four weeks I encouraged different congregations to identify some of the devil's lies in their lives and have a good belly laugh. Whilst congregations were laughing, I decided to laugh at my GP's prognosis. The result of my laughter was that the backache disappeared and over the intervening years I have dug vigorously on my allotment, moved four tons of soil, rocks, paving stones from my front garden to the back garden (breaking my wheelbarrow in the process) building a patio and a beautiful rockery with rock pools, all perfectly free of pain.

Medical research has shown that laughing can help to:

Lower blood pressure.
Slow the pulse rate.
Reduce stress hormones.
Increase muscle flexion.
Boost immune function by raising levels of infection – fighting T cells and disease fighting proteins called Gamma-interferon and B-cells, which produce disease fighting antibodies.
Trigger the release of endorphins, the blood's natural pain killers.
Enhance memory and learning abilities.
Produce a general sense of well-being.
Bring a sense of unity into a group situation.
All these effects can last for eight to twelve hours.

Somebody once said, if you want a good laugh have a good look in the mirror. So, tomorrow morning, start the day by looking in the mirror and you are bound to have a good day! That is why warthogs and tortoises, live so long.

Barbara Johnson, the American Christian author, said,

> Laughter is like changing a baby's diaper. It does not permanently solve the problem, but it makes things more acceptable.

Charles E Jones in his book *Life is Tremendous* said,

> Laughter is the surplus of life, it's the bubbling over of emotions, a kind of spasm of exuberance; a delight that makes the thorax cackle.

Why should we laugh?

1. **Because God's truth is far more powerful than the devil's lies.** It is the truth that sets you free! The truth of God's word is so powerful, so unchanging, so life creating, so amazing that creation rose in form complete by His whisper, and to dare even to consider giving credence to the devil's word is preposterous, laughable.

2. **Because God sits in heaven.** Jesus taught us to pray *Your Kingdom come, Your will be done on earth as it is in heaven.* If God is sitting in heaven laughing in derision at His enemy's words and we are told to ask that what is happening in heaven should happen on earth, we should join in the laughter.

3. **Christ is seated because He has finished the work.** The devil may speak and plan what he likes, but Jesus has finished His work – He has won! *"He was received up into heaven and sat down at the right hand of God," Mark 16:20. All His enemies were under His feet.*

4. **Because Jesus said, *"Whatever the Father does, the Son also does in like manner,"*** *John 5:19.* If Jesus does what the Father does, and we are in Christ and called to walk in His footsteps, then it should follow that we also sit in Heavenly places and laugh.

5. **Because we are seated with Christ in heavenly places.** *"God raised us up together in the heavenly places in Christ Jesus," Ephesians 2:6.* We are people of the horizon, where heaven and earth meet. Sitting with Him, we should laugh with Him. The Psalmist sings, *"You shall tread upon the lion and the cobra: The young lion and the serpent you shall*

trample underfoot", Psalm 91:13. Paul adds, *"The God of peace will swiftly pound Satan to a pulp under your feet!" Romans 16:20 tPt.*

Reader, have you heard any good lies lately, that you can have a good laugh about? First repent of ever entertaining such rubbish for a single minute, and then laugh them to scorn uproariously. The more I soak myself in God's amazing life giving Word, the more I find myself chuckling at the devil's banal, inane, pathetic statements.

We are told that children laugh on average 400 times per day, whilst adults just 15 times. Who was it who said, "Unless you become as little children…"?

It is time in church to flex our laughter muscles!

***H**e who kisses the joy as it flies*
Lives in eternity's sunrise.
William Blake

15

The Joy of Heaven

How divinely full of glory and pleasure shall that hour be when all the millions of mankind that have been redeemed by the blood of the Lamb of God shall meet together and stand around Him, with every tongue and every heart full of joy and praise! How astonishing will be the glory and the joy of that day when all the saints shall join together in one common song of gratitude and love, and of everlasting thankfulness to this Redeemer! With that unknown delight, and inexpressible satisfaction, shall all that are saved from the ruins of sin and hell address the Lamb that was slain, and rejoice in His presence!

Isaac Watts

No one can begin to understand or comprehend the joys of heaven. It is like a fish in a pond or ocean trying to explain to another fish what life is like beyond the surface of the water, it would not have the first idea, it is another dimension way beyond its comprehension. Nevertheless, we exceedingly rejoice in the little we do have revealed to us in scripture and the inner witness of our hearts.

As a Pastor of three different congregations over a period of some twenty-eight years, I have attended the deathbed of many a church member. Thankfully, most had a real deep faith in Jesus. Some such scenes have been extremely sad as loved ones have relinquished their husband, wife or close relative into the hands of God. Others have been such triumphant, almost joyous occasions as their hopes rise to their entrance into heaven, "sweeping through the gates of the new Jerusalem, washed in the blood of the Lamb."

I have often remarked at funerals of believers who had enjoyed such a wonderful relationship with the Lord in this life, "How can we deny them the joy of meeting those who have gone on before them? Most importantly, how can we deny them the joy of being in the presence of their precious Lord and Saviour, and join in the triumphant victory song and hear the Father say, 'Well done my good and faithful servant?'"

The Apostle Paul cries,

> *The sufferings of this present time are not worthy to be compared with the glory that shall be revealed in us.*
>
> *Romans 8:18.*

And again,

> *Eye has not seen, nor ear heard, nor have entered into the heart of man the things which God has prepared for those that love Him.*
>
> *1 Corinthians 2:9.*

As our bodies begin to wind down with old age or through serious sickness, when what the writer of Ecclesiastes says are, *"the difficult days...the years when you say, 'I have no pleasure in them'," Ecclesiastes 12:1,* what joy is ours, when at last, we are free from the shackles of these frail bodies and become gloriously whole. I sometimes wonder when we read that Jesus wept at the tomb of Lazarus, before He raised Lazarus back to life, if He not only identified with the grief of the sisters, but wept for Lazarus, because He was calling him back from the glories of heaven to the troubles of this life? Oh, to see Him as He is and to be like Him!

DL Moody said,

> If you put a piece of iron in the fire, it very soon loses its dark colour, and becomes red and hot like the fire, but it does not lose its iron nature. So the soul in heaven becomes bright with God's brightness, beautiful like God's beauty, pure with God's purity, and warm like the glow of His perfect love, and yet remains a human soul.

We are told little of life in eternity, probably because it is way beyond our tiny minds to comprehend, but we are told there will be no sorrow or crying, only perfection in the joyous presence of the Trinity and angelic host; and as life lived in His Presence on this earth is such joy unspeakable, in spite all our imperfections, we cannot doubt that our joys down here will be multiplied many times over in heaven.

There is a land of pure delight,
Where saints immortal reign;
Infinite day excludes the night,
And pleasures banish pain.

Joy does not simply happen to us.
We have to choose joy and
keep choosing it every day.
Henri Nouwen

16

A Decision to be Made

This is the day the Lord has made; we will rejoice and be glad in it.
Psalm 118:24

From the moment we wake in the morning until we go to sleep at night, we make decisions. When the alarm goes off in the morning, we choose whether to rise up or have another ten minutes and then panic to get dressed, eat our breakfast and go to work. We choose what clothes to put on, how we make up our face or trim our beard. We have choices what to have for breakfast, or to go without. We get on a bus and hopefully can choose where we sit, get on a train and choose which end of the train to scramble on board. Choose whether to buy a sandwich or not or what to have for lunch. What attitude you take towards your fellow workers. Choices, choices, choices…

The psalmist sings, *"This is the day the Lord has made"*. Every day is a gift from God, and we have a choice. We can complain, and if we do, we are focusing on ourselves and what we like or dislike, or we can make a choice to devote ourselves not to our own happiness but making God happy.

Some who read this book might say, "Well, being happy is alright for some people, but by nature, I am not a joyful person." That would be like saying, "I'm not a loving person." We would have to say to you, "What about God's command to love?" God is giving you and I the power and the ability to become abundantly joyful, it is a muscle that God wants to develop in us all.

As we know, the Apostle Paul was in prison with little hope of release when he wrote *"Rejoice in the Lord always"*. His circumstances did not dictate his joy, his focus did! He made a choice and so can we, it all depends on our focus.

> Resolve to keep happy and your joy shall form an invincible host against difficulties.
>
> Helen Keller

A letter to Donatus from St Cyprian in 2nd century

> This seems a cheerful world Donatus, when I view it from this fair garden, under the shadow of these vines.
>
> But if I climbed a high mountain and looked out over the wide lands, you know what I would see? Brigands on the roads, pirates on the high seas, in the amphitheatre men murdered to please the applauding crowds. Under all roofs, misery and selfishness.
>
> It is really a bad world, Donatus, an incredibly bad world. Yet, in the midst of it, I have found a quiet holy people.
>
> They have discovered a joy which is a thousand times better than any pleasure of this sinful life. They are despised and persecuted, but they care not. They have overcome the world.
>
> These people, Donatus, are Christians and I am one of them.

A Word for Someone Today

"Your sorrow shall be turned into joy."
John 16:20

Come, my heart, cheer up! In a little while I shall be as glad as I am now gloomy. Jesus tells me that by a heavenly alchemy my sorrow shall be turned into joy. I do not see how it is to be, but I believe it, and I begin to sing by way of anticipation. This depression of spirit is not for long. I shall soon be up among the happy ones who praise the Lord day and night, and there I shall sing of the mercy which delivered me out of great afflictions.

CH Spurgeon

Books and Resources by Brian and Vanessa Richardson

The Best of Brian

By Brian Richardson

Brian Richardson has been in Christian ministry for more than sixty years and during that time has garnered a wealth of experience, material, jokes and illustrations that have enriched the way he communicates with congregations and listeners in many cultures.

This book is a collection of the many gems he has accumulated that could be used as a thought for the day, but more importantly a source book for preachers and speakers, hence an extensive subject index.

Don't Quit Now! Go For Your Dreams

By Brian and Vanessa Richardson

From his rich experience of well over 50 years of ministry in many parts of the world, Brian shares in this book some important principles in life – with more than a sprinkling humour – that have helped keep him on track living the Kingdom life.

Vanessa too tells something of her story and how she has held on to her God-given dreams until, by God's grace, they became a reality.

Brian and Vanessa were married in 1993 and have a daughter Anna. They launched Liberation Ministries in October 1999 and since then have ministered in conferences and churches in the UK, Arab Emirates, South America, USA, India, Europe and Eastern Europe.

Your Kingdom Come – The Now And The Not Yet!

By Brian Richardson

A look at the Kingdom of Solomon and how it foreshadows the Kingdom of Christ. *'Your Kingdom come, Your will be done on earth as it is in heaven,'* Matthew 6:10. What do we expect to see when we pray 'Your Kingdom come?'

This book is also available in French.

Now You Do It! A Challenge to Plant New Churches

By Brian Richardson

The heart of this book is to challenge mature Christians and congregations to church plant. It is also designed to encourage and give direction to those who may be considering the possibilities of church planting, to go for it!

It takes you on a journey from why we need to open new churches, to the actual launching of a bouncing baby church. On the way, we take a realistic look at our own potential, and then follow the process of conception to birth of a new church.

Spicing the story with humour, Brian shares from his own personal experience and that of the London City Church (that has planted more than 150 congregations over a 15 year period), the different models that can be undertaken.

Also available in French and Bulgarian.

The Dance

By Vanessa Richardson

This CD takes you on a dance from high praise to the very heart of God and then on to being part of His Warrior Bride.

There are songs of intimate worship and aggressive praise where you can sing along with Vanessa and her excellent band.

BREAKOUT!

An Instrumental Album

By Vanessa Richardson

The words of scripture have the wonderful ability to turn our lives around, set us free and lead us into our true destiny.

In this CD Vanessa seeks to interpret on the keyboard, backed by guitar and percussion, specific passages of scripture to take us on a journey through music and touch our spirits in a different way.

Encounter CD

An Instrumental Album by Vanessa Richardson

God is calling His Bride into greater depths of intimacy with Him. This CD is an invitation to come away with Him into the secret place and find rest, refreshing, healing and restoration in His presence and to experience His love, strength and joy as you run with Him in His purposes.

The Warrior Bride

By Vanessa Richardson

Prophetic Warfare Praise and Intimate Worship

A powerful and biblically based book on changing the spiritual atmosphere through the power of praise and worship to advance the Kingdom of God. Vanessa has a wealth of experience and spiritual insight garnered through years of practical ministry which she shares in a wise and user-friendly way to help worship leaders and others looking for dynamic spiritual breakthrough.

All resources are available to buy from
www.liberationministries.co.uk